# I AM PHOENIX

*Poems for Two Voices*

# I AM PHOENIX

## Poems for Two Voices

### PAUL FLEISCHMAN

*illustrated by Ken Nutt*

*Harper & Row, Publishers*

Library of Congress Cataloging in Publication Data
Fleischman, Paul.
  I am phoenix.
  "A Charlotte Zolotow book."
  Summary: A collection of poems about birds to be read
aloud by two voices.
  1. Birds—Juvenile poetry.  2. Dialogues.
3. Children's poetry, American.  [1. Birds—Poetry.
2. American poetry]  I. Nutt, Ken, 1951–    ill.
II. Title.
PS3556.L422812 1985       811′.54        85-42615
ISBN 0-06-021881-9
ISBN 0-06-021882-7 (lib. bdg.)

Designed by Constance Fogler
3  4  5  6  7  8  9  10

For Charlotte, *rara avis*

# CONTENTS

# NOTE

The following poems were written to be read aloud by two readers at once, one taking the left-hand part, the other taking the right-hand part. The poems should be read from top to bottom, the two parts meshing as in a musical duet. When both readers have lines at the same horizontal level, those lines are to be spoken simultaneously.

# I AM PHOENIX

*Poems for Two Voices*

# Dawn

---

At first light the finches
are flitting about the trees

               Flittering

fluttering

               flit

purple finches

               flit

Fluttering

               flittering

fly

               painted finches

fly.

               Weaver finch
               goldfinches

Weaver finch

goldfinches

finches

flit

brown-capped rosy finch

flutter

flit

finches.

Cassin's finch

house finches

flit

finches

flit

flutter

flit

flutter

flit

finches.

# *Morning*

One waxwing's wakened

two

two

rails have risen

three

three

teal

four

four

storks

five

five

stilts

six

six

California condors

seven sleek

seven sleek

trumpeter

swans

eight scaups

        nine snipes

ten shrikes

twelve         twelve

        rufous-sided towhees

fifteen         fifteen

magnificent         magnificent

frigatebirds         frigatebirds

twenty terns

        thirty-five

dazzling         dazzling

        lazuli buntings

fifty ruffs

        sixty wrens

seventy-seven

sea gulls         sea gulls

        saviors of

Salt Lake City         Salt Lake City

eighty grouse

        ninety grebes

one hundred         one hundred

chickadees!         chickadees!

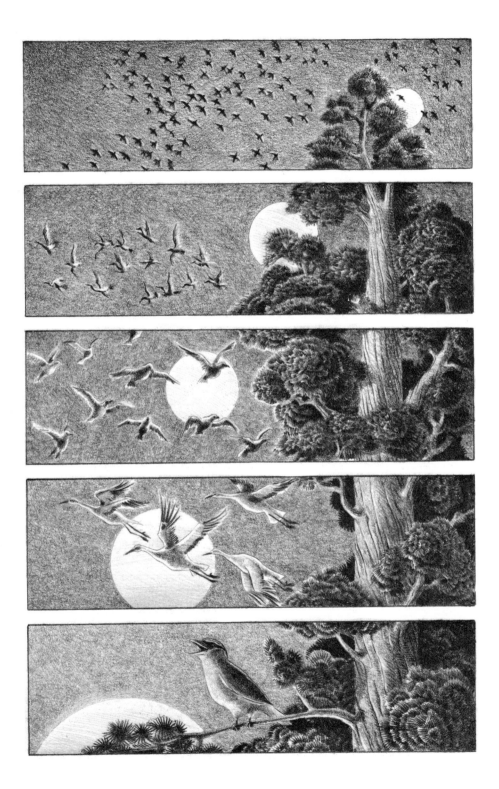

# The Wandering Albatross

Behold the wandering
albatross!
Roaming the lonely
oceans

Believed to bear
the souls of lost
mariners

wandering albatross
Men lost to
storms and sharks

Behold the wandering
albatross!

albatross
wandering

wandering
Sailors swept overboard
wandering albatross

albatross roaming

arisen

a-soaring

Albatross!
Wandering
albatross
Wandering
wandering
albatross!

albatross roaming
The shipwrecked

The storm-drowned

Albatross!
Wandering
ceaselessly
journeying

Wandering
albatross!

# *The Actor*

I
seem
            seem
            a shrike

I
ape
            ape
            the gull

I
sing just like
            sing just like
            the cardinal.
            I
mimic
            mimic
coots

            I
mirror
            mirror
crows

imitate
the orioles.
I
copy

I
echo

I know by heart

But all of that

sham

is what
I *am.*

I
imitate

copy
wrens

echo
owls
I know by heart
the catbird's calls.

is simply
sham
For a mockingbird

I *am.*

# The Watchers

Overhead vultures fly

Overhead vultures fly

Peregrine falcons fly

Peregrine falcons fly

Pigeon hawks

Pigeon hawks
sparrow hawks
red-tailed hawks
sharp-shinned hawks

sparrow hawks
red-tailed hawks
sharp-shinned hawks

circling
Black hawks
slowly circling
Marsh hawks

Black hawks

Marsh hawks
peering

down

down

ground

great

interest.


at the

ground

with

great

interest.

# The Passenger Pigeon

We were counted not in

thousands

nor

millions

but in
*billions.*

*billions.*

We were numerous as the

stars

stars

in the heavens

As grains of
sand

sand

at the sea

As the

buffalo

buffalo

on the plains.

When we burst into flight

we so filled the sky

that the

sun

sun

was darkened

and

day

day

became dusk.

Humblers of the sun

Humblers of the sun

we were!

we were!

The world

inconceivable

inconceivable

without us.

Yet it's 1914,

and here I am

alone

alone

caged in the Cincinnati Zoo,

the last

of the passenger pigeons.

# *The Common Egret*

common

Common!

As if to be so white that

snow

clouds

that milk

rates as ordinary.

They call us
common
egrets.

The injustice!

snow
is filled with envy
clouds
consumed with spite
that milk
should seem molasses

Gold

Gold

should be so slandered

diamonds

diamonds

scorned as worthless

rubies

rubies

spurned

if common

egrets

egrets

are but

*common.*

*common.*

# The Phoenix

---

I am Phoenix

Phoenix
everlasting!
I am Phoenix!

Immortal
eternal.
I live in
Arabia

eagle
My feathers are
scarlet,
purple,

I am Phoenix
the fire-bird!
Phoenix

I am Phoenix!
Immortal
eternal
undying.

Arabia
I'm as large as an
eagle

scarlet,

golden.

one

there have never been more.
I am my own
daughter
granddaughter
great-granddaughter
I was

will be
my gravedigger.

I gather up twigs of
sweet-smelling spices
and build a nest
on the top of a palm.

Then I wait for noon—

fire
I flap my wings

purple.
There is but
one
Phoenix—

I am my own
mother
grandmother
great-grandmother.
I was
my own midwife,
will be

For each time I discover
I'm becoming old

sweet-smelling spices

I climb inside.

and when the sun's hot as
fire

till the twigs beneath me
burst

burst
into flames

which I fan
with my wings
and fan

which I fan
with my wings
and fan
till the fire

and I

are no more.

Eight days pass.
The ashes cool.

Eight days pass.

Then, on the ninth day

in the morning,

at dawn,

just as the sun

rises in the east

*I rise*
from the ashes
and fly upward—

*I rise*

a

new

new
Phoenix,

my own
mother
grandmother
great-grandmother
and on
and on
until the end of time.

daughter
granddaughter
great-granddaughter

and on
until the end of time.

# *Warblers*

Warblers
warbling

Nashville
warblers

Townsend's
Myrtle
Mourning
Wilson's
warblers

Yellow-
throated

Warblers
warbling

Nashville
warblers

Townsend's
Myrtle
Mourning
Wilson's
warblers

Yellow-
throated

Chestnut-
sided

Dozens
of them

Each one
different.


Hooded
warblers


Hermit
warblers


Bachman's
Brewster's
Blue-winged warblers
warbling.

Chestnut-
sided

Dozens
of them

Each one
different.
Hooded
warblers

Hermit
warblers

Bachman's
Brewster's

Blue-winged warblers
warbling.

# The Cormorant's Tale

"As free as a bird"

And I choke when I hear it

I'm an old cormorant
That's my man
with the rope

That circles my throat.
Like all cormorants

The skill's in my bones

"As free as a bird"
I've heard my man say

Consider my case.
I'm an old cormorant



Attached to the ring

Like all cormorants
At catching fish I excel

As my owner knows well.

It's a cormorant's life
To dive down—as right now.

        It's a cormorant's life

        I spot a fish and I seize it

I'm a practiced sea-fowl.
But I'm a caught cormorant

        But I'm a caught cormorant
        —Not the first nor the last—

And the rings
round our necks

        Stop us eating our catch.

Just to taste is our fate
Though our stomachs
are sore

        Just to taste is our fate

        But *they* take the fish

Then we dive after more.
I'm a cormorant, yes

        I'm a cormorant, yes
        And I'll tell you my wish:

To be free and unfettered—
As free as a fish.

        As free as a fish.

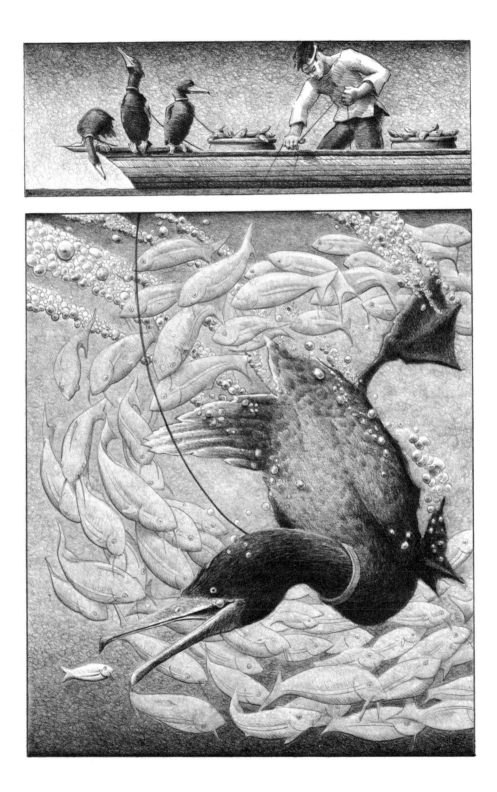

# *Sparrows*

---

Sparrows everywhere
There's sparrows
everywhere
They're
squabbling
flitting
singing
Sharp-tailed

Henslow's

Lincoln's

Sparrows everywhere
There's sparrows
everywhere
They're
flitting
singing
squabbling

found in marshes

note white eye-ring

fond of thickets

( 35 )

Vesper

Sparrows everywhere
They're
flying
chirping
flirting

feeds on insects

sings in flight

bird of brushland

found at dunes from
Cape Cod south to Georgia.
Sparrows
every-
where there's
squabbling
flitting
singing
sparrows

white tail feathers
visible while perching.
Sparrows everywhere
They're
flirting
flying
chirping
Seaside

Cassin's

Clay-colored

Ipswich

Sparrows
every-
where there's
squabbling
sparrows
flirting

every-
where there's
sparrows
everywhere.

flying
chirping
sparrows
everywhere.

# Doves of Dodona

In the country called Greece
We are doves of Dodona

We are doves of Dodona
Near the peak
called Tomarus

All-fathoming birds
Stood the town
called Dodona
Wise doves of Dodona

All-fathoming birds

Wise doves of Dodona
Where our cooing
for thousands of years
has been heard.

We still perch in the oaks
Sacred oaks of Dodona

Sacred oaks of Dodona
Where the oracle lived

In the holy grove
There the prophetess stood
Ancient trees of Dodona

She pondered their questions
We are doves of Dodona

Unpuzzling birds
We answered with cooing
Sage doves of Dodona

We disclosed dying days
Oracle of Dodona

Dweller among trees
Told the outcomes of wars
Priestess of Dodona

In the holy grove

Ancient trees of Dodona
And received those
who sought
what the future might hold.

We are doves of Dodona
Then posed them to us
Unpuzzling birds

Sage doves of Dodona
Which only she knew
how to translate
to words.

Oracle of Dodona
Answered questions of love
Dweller among trees

Priestess of Dodona
Till Dodona
was abandoned
and the questions ceased.

In the country called Greece
We are doves of Dodona

All-fathoming birds
Stood the town
called Dodona
Wise doves of Dodona

We are doves of Dodona
Near the peak
called Tomarus
All-fathoming birds

Wise doves of Dodona
Where our cooing
for thousands of years
has been heard.

# Dusk

---

swifts and swallows
Snapping up insects
swifts and swallows.

Barn swallows
swifts and swallows
Cliff swallows
cave swallows
swifts and swallows

swallows
swift swallows
swift swallows

At dusk there are swallows
swifts and swallows

swifts and swallows.
Barn swallows
bank swallows
swifts and swallows

Cliff swallows
swifts and swallows
Swift and all-swallowing
swallows

swift swallows

swift swallows

swift swallows

swift swallows

swift swallows.

swift swallows

swift swallows

swift swallows.

# *Whip-poor-will*

Whip-poor-will
Will who?
Whip-poor-will

Whip-poor-will
But why?
Whip-poor-will

Whip-poor-will

Hawk told crow
down below

whip-poor-will

Whip-poor-will

Whip-poor-will
Will Grime.
Whip-poor-will

Whip-poor-will
His crime.

He stole a stallion,
witnessed by a hawk high up.

whip-poor-will
Crow told owl
in an oak

Owl told thrush
in a bush

           whip-poor-will

           Thrush told flea

Flea told dog

           Dog told master

Whip           Whip

poor           poor

Will.          Will.

# *Owls*

---

Sun's down,

Sky's dark,

Loons sleeping

Larks sleeping
Black night

Black night
for them,

Bright noon
for owls.

Bright noon

Barn owls

(siskins sleeping)

Barred owls

(phoebes dreaming)
Screech owls

Screech owls

are

           lis-

           ten-

are        ing

lis-

ten-

ing        are

           lis-

           ten-

           ing

Spotted owls

           (sleeping cranes)

Saw-whet owls

           (dreaming quail)

Elf owls        Elf owls

           are

           call-

           ing

are        out

call-

ing

out        are

           call-

           ing

| Great gray owls | Great gray owls |
| are | |
| calling | calling |
| out | |
| into the night. | into the night. |